ABOUT THE AUTHOR

Spoz is an award winning performance poet, singer / songwriter, film maker, playwright and is the poet-in-residence at Birmingham City FC. He has been seen on BBC and Central Television, has written for and been heard on ... BBC Radio Four, Radio Five Live, Radio West Midlands, Radio Coventry & Warwickshire and Capital Gold. He has performed at the Glastonbury Festival, Shambala Festival, Larmer Tree Festival, Cheltenham Literature Festival, Oxford Literature Festival, Warwick Words Festival, Ledbury Poetry Festival and Wenlock Poetry Festival. He was 'crowned' Birmingham's eleventh poet laureate in October 2006. He continues to work extensively in schools, lifting the appeal of writing and performing poetry to hitherto, unseen heights. He has released two poetry collections for children. "The Day the Earth Grew Hair ... and Other Stuff" and "Spoz's Shorts and the Occasional Long One".

Website: https://spoz.co/
Twitter: @SpozPoet
Facebook: giovanni.s.esposito.5

Spoz
Sometimes Angry

VERVE
POETRY PRESS
BIRMINGHAM

PUBLISHED BY VERVE POETRY PRESS
https://vervepoetrypress.com
mail@vervepoetrypress.com

All rights reserved
© 2019 Giovanni Esposito

The right of Giovanni Esposito to be identified as author of this work has been asserted in accordance with section 77 of the Copyright, Designs and Patents Act 1988.

No part of this work may be reproduced, stored or transmitted in any form or by any means, graphic, electronic, recorded or mechanical, without the prior written permission of the publisher.

FIRST PUBLISHED SEP 2019

Printed and bound in the UK
by Imprint Digital, Exeter

ISBN: 978-1-912565-26-9

Cover art by John Davenport, burnt by Spoz.

To Claudia, Francesca and Zack

CONTENTS

No Whites, No Cats, No English	10
Cake or Death	12
Fifteen	14
My Speech Impediment	16
NHS	18
Ninety Two Year Old, Slightly Racist War Veteran	20
Senza Te (Without You)	22
Without You	24
The Preposterous Gammon Balloon	26
Once Upon a Time In The Wild West Midlands	28
Thin White Duke	31
A Wintery Walk Up The Lickey Hills	34
Are We Nearly There Yet?	36
Only The Dead Dreams of The ASBO Kid	39

The Castle Up The Beacon	42
Endangered Species	44
Football for Palestine	46
Fun	49
Here's to You	51
Il Mio Patrimonio ... Innit? (My Heritage ... Innit?)	53
My Heritage ... Innit?	56
Letter to Birmingham	59
Losing It	64
Valentine's Day in the Jungle	66

Spoz Introduces Davanté Dunkley, Jemima Hughes and Tom McCann

Acknowledgements

Sometimes Angry

No Whites, No Cats, No English

No pussyfooting.
Get that sign up because you're entitled to it,
Confidence in abundance ... like Nike said ... just do it!
But with a sense of arrogant superiority.
Self is your priority, numero uno, feline supremo,
No pink eyes on this albino!
Bad ass and biased like a Bond villain's pet,
You just haven't worked that bit out yet.

Making scents to erect an imagined border,
Top of the pecking order
And prepared to hissy fit about it,
Prepared to kick up shit about it,
Spit a sparrow's feathers out and shout, there is no doubt about it,
Then bring the dead bird back through the catflap,
As, perhaps, some kind of a thoughtful gift?
Or just another sign that you find it hard to coexist.
Less stubborn furballs ... more Joseph Goebels.

You shat upon your own front door mat,
Like the cat that got the cream and didn't want to share,
You still believe nostalgia's dream
Of when you thought you were the cat's whiskers,
Yet conveniently forget the blisters on the fingers
That you stepped on to make your way.
You proudly purr about saving the day ...
You know? The one when the vermin came?
You saw them off, not once, but twice!
No room for the disease carried by these despicable mice.

But you were already infected.
Needed neutering and worming
And now the feral pussies are running riot,
While the Reece Moggies are giving you 'catnip' to sniff on the quiet.

They say that pride comes before a fall, in which case,
You must have been queuing up at Beachy Head for a while now
And I'm not entirely sure how
You've not been splattered on the rocks below,
Though, you always land on your feet so the stories go.

And is it true that you have nine lives?
Eight more than most before you're toast,
Though even then, you'll have 101 uses,
So there'll be no excuses on making a proper contribution to society.
I have it on good authority
(Well, a novelty book by Simon Bond, really),
That, as a stiff, ex-kitty,
Your pencil sharpening skills are a little bit ... shitty.

So, instead of soiling our city
With the crap your noisy neighbour feeds you,
Use the litter tray ... and bury those dirty deeds dude.
Because that's the dirt that breeds you,
That's the dirt that bleeds through,
That's the dirt that needs to be nurtured from your nature
Until the haters concede to celebrating all species,
Don't spread your toxic faeces
Pick up the pieces in this natural habitat
Because nobody should pamper a poisonous pussycat.

Cake or Death

"Cake or death?
It's a simple choice ... cake or death?"
You say.
And on any other day, I'd be bound to agree,
But is there something about death, you're not telling me?
Or is cake all that it's cracked up to be?

You see ... I was pretty convinced of my opinion ...
Evidence suggests that this 'no-brainer' of a question,
Has no vague nuance or suggestion
Of anything but 'cake' being the obvious selection.

So why ask it?

Unless your lying breath is trying to dress up death?
Like it does every day, every week,
To ensure your poor outcome doesn't appear so bleak.
To say that you plan for failure,
Flatters your negative opinion of the masses.
You positively engineer situations
That lead to the frustration and termination
Of the limited mobility classes.

You see ...
If death is your product, then it's quite a hard sell,
There're some careless whispers
You're going to have to dispel,
Quell the rumours that are actually fact,
To keep your destructive record intact.

Marketing tactics of denial and lies,
Disguise the certitude and misery of your purgatorial prize,
White washing of eyes to see a new truth,
That requires no precedent, no testament, no proof.

And the collaborators of death with their media powers,
Will convince the plebs that gas chambers ...
Are actually showers ...
That the silent stench of Novichok
Is the scented smell of flowers ...
And that your final moments,
Will be decades instead of hours.

As you watch those watch towers
Grow taller than the trees,
You will believe they're there to preserve your security,
You will believe there's an enemy
That lurks within,
You will believe that caring is a mortal sin.

So ... why have cake,
When death is as alluring as a porn star's crotch?
Sweeter than lemon drizzle with a hint of butterscotch,
More top-notch than a Rolex watch,
Just make sure you put your 'x' in the right box,
It's your democratic right to want to hunt and kill a fox,
It's your democratic right to take back control at all costs
It's your democratic right for goodness sake,
It's your democratic right to have death ...
Instead of cake.

Fifteen

Fifteen ... and I'm reading a label that says 34C,
Another English lesson and she's sat in front of me,
Like she always is ... three times a week,
Next to her mate, the one who thinks I'm a geek.

Yeah ... whatever.

You see, I used to get a bit excited when we did poetry at school,
Everyone else had their go to setting of "Boring!"...
I guess they thought they were being cool.
You were considered a tool at our 'secondary modern',
For diggin' odes ... well sod 'em ...
I preferred the road less trodden ... or something like that.

There was a chemistry ... an allure in those words and verses,
That was better than girls dressed as naughty maids or nurses ...
Well ... sometimes.
Those sentences and couplets were on the page in black and white,
Constant ... unwavering ... in the day and in the night.
They always stayed the same,
They wouldn't change into different things ...
And at the wrong time of the month ...
They didn't have mood swings.

The poems invited you to 'get stuck in',
They didn't care if you weren't good lookin' ...
The kind of blunt seduction you don't hear when you're being seduced,
'Cause how many girls would say that, if they'd just been intro**duced.**

English became my favourite lesson ... no messin'...
With those answers to questions made to keep you all guessin'.
I would read between the lines to see if the words changed their definition,
I was on a mission ... like Indiana Jones,
Though I was looking for diamonds – not dinosaur bones.

Now, don't get me wrong – I really liked girls
But the one's I liked ...
Well ... they were out of my league, just like she was,
Though I knew she kind of liked me 'cause
She was friendly ... we'd chat and pass the time of day
But I guess I knew she didn't really like me in that way.
But that was okay.
I still thought about the view that I'd get in English classes,
Which goes some way to explain why today ... I'm wearing glasses.

My Speech Impediment

People didn't notice at first.
Either that or they never really cared –
Were they even aware of what they were hearing?
Were their ears impaired or was I ... moderately endearing?

You see ... I couldn't pronounce my "ch" sounds.
That blasted "h" turned my "c's" into raging oceans,
Made plain conversations into painful discourses,
Peppered with agony and ...
... awkward pauses.

Now they say that kids can be cruel ... and some were,
No matter how I tried to deter their taunts,
Their jibes would haunt and chide and choke,
Turning my chat ... into the butts of jokes.
And yeah ... it wasn't just "ch's" that would start the squeeze,
But "j's" and "g's" would leave me crawling on my knees ...
And the occasional "sh" would rob me of my dulcet tones,
Turning pearls of wisdom ...
Into worthless stones.

What should have been the warmth of a steam train's puffing,
Was turned into something like new school shoes scuffing.
And as I grew ... it became as obvious as
A beggar at a wedding reception,
Or blood on a school blazer,
Or a flasher at a children's party.
And there was part of me that didn't care
But a bigger part would see the stares and smirks,
Because sometimes ... that's how a child's brain works.

So I began to consider what I said
Worked out synonyms in my head so I could avoid words like ...
"Church" or "speech" or "children".

Imagine "children" falling from my vocabulary.

And as I trudged my way through high school,
It felt like I was walking my own road to perdition.
The speech police had their batons drawn,
Ready to beat me into submission
And I kept wishing ... for situations to change,
And for when my words ... wouldn't sound so strange.
A process of self editing and filters ensued,
To ensure those crackles were rarely heard ...
"Children" became "kids"
"Church" became "Mass"
And "speech" became "spoken word"

And it was kind of working.
When I occasionally lapsed or the filter failed,
My train of dialogue didn't become derailed,
Giggles were curtailed and to my surprise
I began to realise that it was what I said ...
Rather than the way I said it ... that really mattered.
My preconceived notions were shattered
As I walked back into church,
(Though I've walked past many more since),
Embraced the spoken word
Because speeches won't make themselves
And denying I have a big mouth is as futile as
A futile thing on national futility day.

And yes ... I reclaimed my children too.

NHS

In austere days of hardship and destitution,
The son of a Welsh coal miner dared to dream ...
A service ... a scheme,
That left no one in need.
A leap of faith and a concrete constitution,
That gave a nation's well being a revolutionary solution.

But like many revolutions, it was met with resistance.

Derisory voices of doomed experiments
Echoed then as they do now,
As this was the antithesis of a hierarchy's cash cow.
Society's high brow and so called 'elite'
Began to whine and whinge and bleat
"You can't make a silk purse from a sow's ear!"
But it was blatantly clear ... that we could.

And we did ... sort of.

We "sort of" saved millions of lives that may have been lost,
Had the conservative bean counters said,
"That's just too high a cost".
And while they carped about cost in monetary terms,
We traded in the currency of care,
Rather than considering financial returns.

We "sort of" built a people's empire of salvation,
From every ethnicity, culture and nation,
Magnanimous migration brought us doctors and nurses,
As we continued to sew those "sort of" silk purses.

We "sort of" led the world and we "sort of" still do,
It's no longer survival of the fittest,
It's survival of me and you ... it's true,
The many not the few,
Each one of us touched irrespective of wealth
Rejecting the suggestion of putting profit before health.

So ... when you hear those profiteers whisper,
With the innocence of a virgin's caress,
Don't be caught unawares,
They only care about their shares,
Be aware it's not theirs ...
But everyone's NHS.

Ninety Two Year Old, Slightly Racist War Veteran

... And he looked like such a nice man at first,
With his peacock puffed out Windsor Davis chest
And well rehearsed verse.

As he started to speak, I started to form opinions
That were probably as unfair as his were going to be,
A whiff of duplicity about this war time commentary ...
Or was it just me?

He told us tales of glory disguised as disgust,
A feigned, foreign horror that still chanted,
"Two world wars and one world cup, do - dah ... do - dah"
He started to give himself away behind a medal plumage
Of honour and pride,
His version of history was enabled,
Because he'd been on the winning side.
He laid a thin veil of Wilfred Owen poems, like a wreath,
That he paid lip service to, though never believed,
He told us how he'd wept and grieved for those lost colleagues;
Almost openly sobbed ...
Though I did wonder how many of their widows he'd shagged,
After being de-mobbed.
I wondered if his truth was that of a fisherman's tale,
I wondered if he'd got his coat and medals from the local jumble sale,
I wondered if he'd seen any action at all,
I wondered if he got some kind of satisfaction
Out of making people feel small.

Now that does sound a tad unfair doesn't it?

After all, I'd only met him briefly that evening,
But when someone queues up in the book buying book queue
Not to buy your book, but simply to tell you
How awful your accent is
And how it's made worse by your "bastardised Italian ancestry",
Then forgive me ...
Because sometimes I just don't have the strength
To climb above the bigotry,
Sometimes I just can't see beyond your faux supremacy,
Sometimes situations such as this, twist my melon and boil my piss,
Sometimes I succumb to the will of the devil,
Sometimes ... I feel justified ... in sinking ... to his level ...
Almost.
"Ninety two you say?
That's a very good age isn't it?
You'll be dead soon then?"

No sooner had the words left my mouth,
Celebratory fireworks exploded over head,
A myriad of imaginary anti racist activists, high fived me in ecstasy,
Then punched the air in victory,
Voices unified in their vengeful ferocity.
"That showed him!" said one,
"'Ave that yer bastard!" said another,
Whoops and cheers from another and another and another ...

His weathered face stared back at me,
With the look of a childless surrogate mother,
Who'd just handed over one more sister or brother.
Slowly ...he turned away and left, realising his petty ignorance,
Leaving me behind ... to realise mine.

Senza Te (Without You)

Senza te ...

Sono com' un notturno senza la notte,
Sono stitico senza lassativo per alleviare me stesso,
Sono un vampiro senza il morso,
Adesso ...
Essere senza zanne sarebbe ingrato,
E in una classifica avrei rango meno,
Di un pirata senza una tavola.

Senza te ...

Sono come l'amante inetto sul bordo del dirupo,
Che cambia idea,
Di front'alla bellezza del creato esistenziale,
Basta uno stronzo per spingerlo.
Sono come l'influenza, senza un colpo di tosse,
Com' il "Baywatch" senz' il "Hoff".
Non fare una mossa...
C'è solo tanta soddisfazione nel guardare le ragazze,
Che corrono al rallentatore.
Sono com'un bambino bruciato dal sole, senza la lozione.

Senza te ...

Sono com' un cristiano "rinato" che viene colpito da un fulmine,
Un treno fantasma che non fa paura,
Sono come il bambino vittima di bullismo nel parco,
Che rifiuta di piangere davanti agli amici,
Per paura di rendersi conto che questi sono i bei tempi.
È triste...
Io sono com' un bidone di merda di cane, senza la merda di cane,
Il l'ultimo biscotto nella scatola di biscotti,
Un peccatore che ha perso la volontà di peccare.

Senza te ...

Sono come Stephen Hawking senza il suo linguaggio robotico,
Un' armellina senza la pesca,
Un tenore che proprio non tocca il "do" acuto di "Nessun Dorma".
Tu sei il pollo nel mio Korma,
Il vapore nella mia sauna quando siamo seduti nudi,
Senza te ... io sono la conseguenza sprégevole del cibo ...
Solo merda.

Without you

Without you ...

I'm like a nocturne without the night
Like a constipation sufferer without the laxative to shite
A vampire without the bite,
That's right ...
Being fangless would be thankless
And in a league table I would rank less
Than a pirate what is plankless

Without you ...

I'm like the feckless lover at Beachy Head
Who changes his mind
When confronted by the existential beauty of creation
Only to have some fucker push him off.
I'm like the flu without a cough ...
Baywatch without 'The Hoff' ...
Don't scoff ...
There's only so much satisfaction one can gleam
From watching girls running in slow motion
I'm like a sunburnt child without the calamine lotion.

Without you ...

I'm like a banker without a bonus
A charmless Harry Potter dispersing 'Dementors' with no 'petronas'
A bosom without the 'o' – ness
Rendering it the British School of Motoring
Oh to bring your radiance back
And sack this freshness that I lack
You're like a generous sprinkling of 'Shake and Vac'.

Without you ...

I'm like a born again Christian that gets struck down by lightnin'
A ghost train that's not frightenin'
I'm like the bullied child in the playground
Refusing to cry in front of his peers
For fear of realising that this is playtime for him
It's grim ...
I'm like a dog shite bin without any dog shite in
The last biscuit in the biscuit tin
A sinner who's lost the will to sin

Without you ...

I'm like Stephen Hawking without the speak and spell speech
A pith without the peach
A tenor who just can't reach
That high 'C' in 'Nessun Dorma'
You're the chicken in my Korma
The steam in my sauna when we're sitting in the nude
Without you ... I'm the contemptible consequence of food...
Just shit.

The Preposterous Gammon Balloon

He can't suffer sense of humour loss, 'cause he's not got one,
He thinks his views on immigration are always spot on,
Writes a lot of 'Facebook' posts with the CAPS LOC ON!
'Cause he's the preposterous gammon balloon.

He likes to laugh at refugee boats when the sea gets choppy,
His social media punctuation and spelling's proper sloppy,
He's been seen flashing a "seig heil" whilst wearing a poppy,
The preposterous gammon balloon.

He may look a bit like Fred West, or even Ian Huntley,
Finds it impossible to express himself in any other way but bluntly,
He takes the fun out of 'fundamentalist' and puts the first syllable
    in 'country',
Hideously preposterous gammon balloon.

He stands next to Oswald Moseley pictures, to learn stuff via osmosis,
The mere mention of asylum seekers, can lead to a near thrombosis,
If only he were a rabbit, so we could bring on some myxomatosis,
For the preposterous gammon balloon.

The foreign aid budget leaves him bewildered, raging and crazed,
Believes Enoch Powell and Piers Morgan are icons to be praised,
'Cause they are gammon, just like him ... just a little bit honey glazed,
What a preposterous gammon balloon.

"Just get on with it!" he screams when the Brexshit hits the fan,
"Look at all those PC snowflakes ... man up and be a man!"
As the nation jumps out of the frying pan and into ... another frying pan,
With the preposterous gammon balloon.

He prays at the church of Tommeh Robinson, the EDL and Britain First,
Drinks a pint of German lager to quench his British thirst,
Tell him Muslims are moving in next door and watch his eyeballs burst!
The preposterous gammon balloon.

Once Upon a Time In The Wild West Midlands

Once upon a time in the wild West Midlands,
A young man called Imran helps Margaret across the street,
Carries her stuff as she shuffles her feet to the other side,
"Take care" said Imran,
"Thanks bab" she replies.
And in that moment, Smethwick smiles,
Walmley feels warmer and Stourbridge sighs.
And it's no surprise when you realise
That the wild West Midlands ain't so ... well ... wild.
But we've got teeth,
You can see them when we grin,
We've got mats at our doors to welcome you in
To our neck of the woods ...
Yeah ... we've got rainbows in our neighbourhoods.

Yet this may contradict the narrative
That some gammon faced pricks don't want to see the merit of.
Gagging to be triggered by 'mazel tov' and 'ni hao',
'Marhaba', 'dzien dobry', 'wha gwan' ... and 'ciao'.
You see ... we have neighbours who help neighbours
Of different cultures and nations,
A common bond of humanity without confrontation.
And with a little patience we begin to see
The beauty in our diversity.

Once upon a time in the wild West Midlands,
Theatres of dreams, galleries and libraries
Paint a legacy of art and creativity
That nobody fully understands ...
Yet they see sunsets from far away lands,
Hear heavy metal guitar riffs from plastic tipped right hands.
Steel pulses from Reggae bands and a techno loop ...
CBSO symphonies float like croutons in a musical soup,
Seasoned with Bhangra beats and The Spencer Davis Group.
Take an extra scoop, like we did from one of many Genos,
Because he knows, when Eileen's got poorly bambinos...
Ice cream is always better than Venos.

Once upon a time in the wild West Midlands,
A young, vibrant generation,
Set sail on ships of elbow grease and education.
All manner of youthful variations ... some big, some clever,
Though all blessed with the gift of a blossoming endeavour ...
And with a cheeky "whatever" ... every son, every daughter,
Will shine brighter than the diamonds
In the Jewellery Quarter.
And though some of the science police will tell them
That the brightness is reflected light,
They won't get bogged down with detail or get distracted ... right?
Distracted by those who seek to bring them down
So they can feel superior,
As they shout 'snowflake' at the shat upon millennials,
Because, back in their day, they suffered far too many falls
To allow anyone else to climb,
Far too busy playing 'King Rat' in their shitty pantomime.

Once upon a time in the wild West Midlands,
Theatres of dreams, galleries and libraries
Paint a legacy of art and creativity
That nobody fully understands ...
Yet they see sunsets from far away lands,
Hear heavy metal guitar riffs from plastic tipped right hands.
Steel pulses from Reggae bands and a techno loop ...
CBSO symphonies float like croutons in a musical soup,
Seasoned with Bhangra beats and The Spencer Davis Group.
Take an extra scoop, like we did from one of many Genos,
Because he knows, when Eileen's got poorly bambinos...
Ice cream is always better than Venos.

Once upon a time in the wild West Midlands,
A young, vibrant generation,
Set sail on ships of elbow grease and education.
All manner of youthful variations ... some big, some clever,
Though all blessed with the gift of a blossoming endeavour ...
And with a cheeky "whatever" ... every son, every daughter,
Will shine brighter than the diamonds
In the Jewellery Quarter.
And though some of the science police will tell them
That the brightness is reflected light,
They won't get bogged down with detail or get distracted ... right?
Distracted by those who seek to bring them down
So they can feel superior,
As they shout 'snowflake' at the shat upon millennials,
Because, back in their day, they suffered far too many falls
To allow anyone else to climb,
Far too busy playing 'King Rat' in their shitty pantomime.

Thin White Duke

You came across the Universe and fell to earth,
Gave birth to a thin white Duke from a plastic soul,
With a cigarette in hand.
You killed the man,
Broke up the band,
Then time took the cigarette and put it in your mouth.
The side effects of the cocaine made you uncouth,
But what in the world could you do?
Especially in those golden years?

Lovers were brought to tears as you threw darts in their eyes
And it was no surprise that when you tried to eulogise,
You borrowed wild words from the wind,
Cynically grinned as you opened doors and pulled some strings,
When all you meant to say was "stay".

Because this was a new you,
A kind of broken and hollow you,
A looser, hard to swallow you
And you could never really tell,
When somebody wanted something you wanted too.

Class A benders left your world developing in monochrome,
Colourless and fascist and a long way from home,
You'd traded London for Los Angeles,
Slit the Catholic throat of the laughing gnome
And climbed out of a coned spaceship of Styrofoam.
The Starman had gone;

You'd been dancing again with John
And the blue guitar and orange mullet that had drawn me in,
Had sung their swan songs.
Ronno's gold top had been taken to 10th avenue with Trevor,
While Woody upped sticks to another endeavour.

But you were still my pin-up.
You watched Emily play with all the madmen
And then became one,
A rock 'n' roll suicide you almost couldn't abstain from,
Crashing the train that you'd put Aladdin Sane on,
Yet another one of your changes
That you had to face the strain on.

You traded Twiggy for a skull on a cracked actor's stage,
Your scheme of things were black and white,
Now cabaret was all the rage.
You painted portraits in flesh while diamond dogs
Howled an Orwellian dystopia ,
Yet this, somehow seemed darker
Like a holiday in Cambodia.

Anyway Mr. Jones, while my twelve year old brain wrestled
With what all this was really about,
My admiration grew and I had no sense of doubt
That your star would continue to rise
And like those swinging boys ... you'd work it out.
So ... thank you for the fantastic voyage
And my creative foundation,
Thank you for your electric eyes and the anger of looking back,
Thank you for a legacy of brutal inspiration,
Thank you my prettiest star,
You shining star of black.

I can still (vaguely) remember seeing David Bowie on "Top of the Pops" in 1972. I was eight years old. He was ace and I've been a massive fanboy ever since. This year, Rick Sanders (a top poet based in the Black Country) put a project together called "PoArtry" (see what they did there?), which combined visual art with poetry, by pairing poets and visual artists together to see what they came up with ... the poet to be inspired by a piece of art by the visual artist and vice versa. I had the great fortune to be paired up with Kirk Andrews (www.kirkandrewsart.com), who created amazing charcoal portraits of pop and rock stars. When I saw "The Thin White Duke" in his gallery, I was smitten. Check out his website for his response to my poem "Fun".

A Wintery Walk Up The Lickey Hills
For Dixon

Tension ... taut like the tight rope walker
Between two towers with no tether.
Together we trudge with visible breaths
Toward the toposcope,
Where the world appears
And opens itself up like a naked lover
With nothing to hide ... yet everything hidden.
And they could all see me,
If they would only look –
As they used to,
When the torch on this beacon was lit,
To warn of bygone terrorists.
The tourists have taken leave.
Tired of turning backs against
Tiny tempests and tumbling temperatures,
Lacking persistence ... of thermal resistance.
They will remain oblivious to the troubadour
That would have walked amongst them,
Jostling with language ...
Wrestling with lines ...
Throwing sticks for his dog,
That one day ... will not be retrieved.

Dixon

Are We Nearly There Yet?

There are always the days we will want to forget ...
... but will sadly remember.

Sliding scales on a downward trend,
From Octobers to Novembers and round the bend to
Groundhogged Yule logs and "we never knew, there'd be,
Nothing new ... new years".

A million resolutions in leu of a revolution,
That may or may not be televised,
Yet needs to be realised, so we can claim the real prize,
Of a righteous constitution,
Get wise and reject the compromised refrain
That you can expect to hear again and again ...
Turn and face the strain ... ch ... ch ... changes
Are what we need
To ensure it's more than just the chosen few ...
Who succeed.
Because the criteria for choice is skewed
And when you allude to wealth being a measure of achievement,
I can see common sense has suffered a bereavement.
And while you may be vehement in your disagreement,
I will take your opinions on board ...
Like a ship's captain takes on board infected rats,
Yeah ... call me a bigot, you fucking fat cats,
Getting morbidly obese as you feed us scraps,
Diverting world attention with fabricated facts.
You know a few bullshit brass tacks

Will get the wide eyed plebs and proles,
Behaving and berating like arseholes.
"It's the immigrants, it's the poles, it's no border controls,
That will bring England the brave to her knees ...
It's asylum seekers, it's refugees!"
As they digest a diet of right wing nob cheese.
Millions stare salivating as privileged classes gorge their arses,
Suckling on an unsustainably swollen breast,
Mother knows best but is repeatedly raped by the beast,
The one percent ...
Triggering a winter of discontent that will last for all seasons,
Where the pursuit of peace is labelled treason ...
And if money is not your God ...
You're considered a heathen.

This well established establishment of yours
Continually skips through revolving doors of plenty,
While our continuous chores leave our bellies empty
Is that how it's meant to be?
You're busy manipulating the subjectivity
Of fairness and equality,
Blatantly dragging out your career's longevity,
Spitting on morality and your personal integrity ...
If you ever had any.
You move the goalposts so often these days,
You've put them on castors,
Anxious dancers for your puppet masters,
Attention diverters from displeasing disasters,
"So sorry we killed and maimed and hurt yer,
But you got in the way of our 'cash converter'!"

I face palm myself so much these days, my cheek's gone red,
Tossing and turning in bed,
While I figuratively and literally pull hair from my head,
Common senses dead or too close to death ...
Even my scrabble tiles keep coming up with "WTF".

So as we drive down the road toward equity,
Through the wind and the rain and the snow
And the kids ask "are we nearly there yet dad?"
"Well kids ... we've a long way to go".

Only the Dead Dreams of the ASBO Kid

As I listen to the radio spouting a lock 'em up mentality,
The right wing reality dawns
With streams of words with no thoughts in the pauses,
Condemning the effects ... though never questioning the causes.
So in a fit of frustration I phone up the station,
To offer my words of measured moderation (yeah...right...)
Words that were meant with the best intent,
Though seemed to fall...lost on the ground ...
So I turned up my volume ...but still no sound,
As my words were met by walls of ignorance ...
So my face folded and frowned.

Now, I know facial expressions don't really work on radio,
But were my words getting through ... in hindsight .... maybe no.
'Cause all I got was short shrift from the presenter's moanin'
And he was only really qualified to do a "football phone in".
Didn't realise that to question the wherefores and whys
Is NOT to justify ... NOT the same as condoning.
And there he was ... prescribing cures and pouring scorn
On conditions that had been left to fester since before I was born.

So, fed up of listening to his incessant shite,
I wound up my words and bid him goodnight ...
That's when it happened ...
All those words, while I was on air, that I wanted to say,
Turned up when I hung up ... ain't it always the way ...

Words that differentiate between disenfranchised and delinquent
Distinguish between unable and unwilling... it's chilling...
As the social mincing machine keeps churning and churning,
Turning lost hope into an unreasonable yearning,
For what society and the media tells them "You must have!",
Or Murdoch's scummy empire will label you a chav and a loser
Consumerism is their drug and they're making you the user
Though never fulfilling what a balanced appetite is all about ...
'Cause shit in ... usually equals shit out.

So the lost boy loots and the lost girl screams
As they clutch and cradle their dying dreams
That are drowning ... drowning faster...
Faster than the last witch that was thrown into the cut
Of the last apathetic disaster.

He stands in the doorway of despair, knowing he's going to go in
As the bouncer looks him up and down
And grins another knowing grin.
He's choking on the right wing rhetoric and vomit
That yesterday's Daily Mail front page had splattered on it.
Quick to judge, quick to anger, quick to reprimand ...
Slow to understand
Corner any animal and it'll always bite your hand,
'Cause that's what he does
And it's what his dad and his dad's dad did ...
They're only the dead dreams of the ASBO kid.

And then tomorrow, in class, if he gets that far,
The cycle starts again ...
The cycle of mental pain ...
The cycle of bad name,
The cycle of shame,

The cycle that can only end when the chain breaks
And the brakes make the wheels stop turning
And start the learning,
Because the next steps might be the one of no return
To pastures greener ... or at least to a pasture with some grass on,
With hopes and dreams to pass on ...
Of pavements with no broken glass on
And who knows ... even a cup of tea and a croissant,
That's been bought and paid for from a local independent retailer,
Rather than a corporate franchise,
Seek the truth ... don't laud the lies,
Let's do up the laces that a failed legacy undid,
One less dead dream ...One less ASBO kid.

The Castle Up the Beacon

I can see your house from here ...
In fact ... I can see all of your houses from here ...
And when the weather's clear
And the sky's as blue as a Saturday afternoon at St. Andrew's,
Win or lose, I will always choose ... this.
I'm your borderland beacon that bore down on you from birth,
Giving Rubery a view like 'Google Earth'
Before you even knew what computers were.

They call me a 'toposcope' these days,
But I will always be your castle ...
More than just a Cadbury treat sat upon this grassy hill,
And from this toppest top it's hard to see
The veins of your rich realities,
Your variety of societies and your diverse nationalities.

Zoomed out up here hides the hustle and hurry of you,
Webbed feet flapping like the clappers,
When all I see is a swan ... but I know what goes on.
I've felt it in the happy skips of inner city children,
I've heard it in the banter of a hundred different languages,
I've smelt it in a thousand trades
Of glass and cars and chocolate,
I've sampled it in spices, samosas and cheese sandwiches.

I've been watching Birmingham
And The Black Country grow, up here,
I can see roads like rivers, ebb and flow, up here,
I've wept with family generations as they come and go, up here,
I've seen the fervent kisses of mistletoe, up here.

I've chuckled at tangled kite strings and clumsy gamboles,
Laughed at pet dog picnic pirates as they plundered ham roles,
I'm the fortress in the forest that you long to get lost in,
I'm the smile on your face ...
I am ace,
I am bostin.

Endangered Species

We're an endangered species ...
Wading through faeces and bent on oblivion.
Craving half chances ... but nobody's giving them,
'Cause we've got out own lives and we're just too busy living them
To be stopping and thinking
About those on the brink and seeing they're our neighbours...

We're gorging ourselves on the fruits of our labours ...
...or as is often the case - someone else's ...
A twisted notion of what real wealth is.
Because some people judge well being by the balance on a bank sheet
And sure, we all want to live and eat ... comfortably,
But be honest with me ...

Who the fuck needs a Range Rover in London?
Unless you're taking it "up the heath" in Hampstead like George Michael,
A 4X4 is better by far than any car or motor cycle.
Trade in your Bentley, part ex your Aston Martin,
If it's a fight you're after then you better stop starting,
'Cause what you call a necessity ... is like a red rag to a bull to me.
These baubles and trinkets are a vulgar obscenity,
They're like a profanity,
That adequately displays your lack of humanity,
It's just vanity ... and it ain't fair.
While your cup runneth over with hundreds,
There are thousands and millions who don't even have cups,
There's something missing, there's no pot to piss in,

Can you unblock your ears 'cause you ain't even listening.
Generations tainted by the media's "dissing"
Disenfranchised
Dismembered
Discriminated
Disremembered

There are countless communities of poor - sods - conned,
Who keep the relative minorities in all - mod - cons,
Their muted cries are louder than bombs
As they fall on deaf eyes and blind ears,
The fat end of the wedge ain't been this fat in years
A society so senseless and desensitised these days,
It makes me want to ... mix up my clichés.

But what's that self righteous quip I hear you say?
About paying the taxes you're asked to pay,
About earning and spending the way that you choose,
About how exploitation's just another tool to use,
About working hard, playing hard every day,
About stepping on fingers to make your way,
About the feckless reaping their just rewards,
But when I tell you that your reasoning's flawed,
You come back with your usual contented retort...
"You're just jealous mate".

Football for Palestine

Months of Sundays have passed us by,
Yet all I see is now,
Where Palestine only drinks
When the Israeli authorities allow,
Because wars are waged by withholding water,
So that livelihoods and livestock
Face the drawn out slaughter of thirst,
Where bouts of manufactured droughts leave a land
Once blessed ... now cursed.

Cursed by the daylight robbery
That runs rampant from the river to the sea,
Cursed by the scorched earth
Of a flash grenade and tear gas spree,
Cursed by a torn out and replanted olive tree
That claims a tortured truth
Yet a multitude of broken cameras
Are inadmissible as proof.

I see makeshift umbrellas against a hard rain
That showers market stalls with debris and disdain,
Rocks and rubbish again and again
Under the IDF's watchful eyes
Yet they're deaf, dumb and blind to the cries
Of victims they're told and have grown to despise,
Hunger strikers facing death
All because of their love of life ...
A bitter, twisted irony in the homeland of the Christ.

So we play the beautiful game with beautiful people,
Who face anxiety and upheaval
From illegal settlements built on stolen land,
Where a call for justice will bring down the heavy hand
Of an apartheid state,
That tries to silence cries of freedom,
That persist and resist and refuse to capitulate.

So, for a short while we raise a smile and reconcile,
That whilst our actions may appear small,
Our solidarity is shared with the kick of a ball,
Our words on the walls that we'd gladly trade for bridges,
Are words for humanity that go beyond religious,
Hold onto your wishes, your dreams, your defiance
Like the words in the anthem of The Small Heath Alliance,
Existence is resistance, let's share the load ...
And keep right on to the end of the road.

Fun

The night is young and so are you,
You've already necked a few,
But like a kiddy in Cadbury World,
You gaze upon the rainbow of delights
And think ... it's going to be one of those nights.

An unattainable cleavage, cleaves the money from your pocket,
For that kaleidoscope of clever juice that fires your rocket,
Don't knock it ...
It's blue, it's pink, it's green, it's clear, it's anyone of these,
It tastes like "Covonia" cough linctus and looks like anti-freeze,
It's cheap at twice the price, you can never pay too much
For the courage it bestows ... albeit dutch.

So you neck a few ... three more than two
And you're good – tall as a tower
Your excess is the access to your own corridor of power.
Like the Don, you're full of offers no one can refuse,
You can't loose – driven by the booze you spot a girl,
Wearing so little she could get arrested,
Give her some chat – but she ain't interested,
She wants a higher return on what she's invested
And it ain't you ... no where near,
So have another beer and a vodka shot,
"I'll come back later when you're hot to trot ..."
What?!
Do people still say that?!
No, it's just your decadence talking ... and it's calling you a twat.

So you neck a few more ... one less than four
And you're good – hard as nails,
You're in a town that never fails to deliver jailbirds for jails.
'Cause you're a dick by day so why be different in the dark,
You're about to become a dog who's bite's worse than his bark.

It's that girl again – that one with next to nothing on – from 'Next'
And you're vexed ... and ...
"Who's that wanker she's with? Look at the way he talks..."
Your fuse is lit ...
You're Guy Fawkes ...
You're fit to burst ...
He's James the First ...

Then, before you know it, you've blown it
The first punch lands twelve hours after you've thrown it.
In with another - he stalls,
In with the boot – he falls,
Down comes the mist, the time bomb's ticking,
His eyes roll, he goes limp but you don't stop kicking.

You see ... one's notion of a good time can vary a lot,
What makes something "fun" and what makes it ... not,
Getting pissed with your mates
May be a source of hilarity,
But at which point does "fun" turn into vulgarity?
It lacks clarity ... it's vague
By whose rule do we measure?
Are all acts of fun designed to give pleasure?
A moment to treasure or a moment of greed,
When self satisfaction surpasses your need.

Here's to You

Here's a little shout out
To the hungry and impoverished labourers,
Who downed tools and trekked a thousand miles
To pick up new ones;
With a hearty new language to chew on, in a new land,
They found and mouthed words to communicate,
In a place they didn't fully understand.

As their swarthy complexions turned ruddy,
After being stood in the British winter for a while,
They learnt to endure in an environment
That could turn a little hostile,
And I'm not just talking about the freezing weather.
Because when their mountains weren't baking in summer,
They were snow capped in winter,
Knee deep treks into the campagnia,
So ... you know ...
They were used to that kind of cold without exception ...
It just took a little more to acclimatise
To a bell end's frosty reception.

Here's a grateful little pat on the back
To all the intrepid adventurers,
Who rode the blows and faced the flak
Of countless shouts of "go back to your own country".
Bless your skin, that must have been as thick as the morons,
These gormless thoughts spawned from.
They saw the numbers, though never understood mathematics,
Their ignorance was tragic,

Blame was their game, scapegoating, their tactics.
Your boats and planes crashed through waves
Of "coming over here, nicking our jobs",
While lazy slobs and bigoted gobs full of shite and sick,
Ate fruit they couldn't be arsed to pick.

Here's a humble "thank you"
To the South African doctor who diagnosed me,
To the Irish lady who made me tea,
To the Asian lady who helped feed me,
To the Chinese junior doctor who lumbar punctured me,
To the windrushed nurse who bathed me
When my limbs had failed.
We laughed and wailed in patois and Brummie,
"It's okay sonny! It look like a penis, just a lickle bit smaller!"
She smiled every time I had to call her,
She had a heart with compassion to build nations on ...
Yet some bastards today, still want to see her gone.

So people, keep coming if you really want to come,
To where all can prosper and not just the few,
Freedom for all and not just for some,
Here's to us all, but especially, to you.

Il Mio Patrimonio ... innit?
(Mi Heritage ... Innit?)

Assomigliare a qualcuno di statura,
Oppure, per catturare una qualità che porta rapimento,
Potrebbe essere classificato come una cosa meravigliosa ...
Forse sei l'immagine di Martin Luther King?
Oppure ... di John Lennon o di Ghandi, di Kate Bush o di Bob Marley
Io? Io sono l'immagine dello splendido ... Joe Pasquale.
Ma va bene perché è un bravo ragazzo,
Quindi non cercare di farmi sentire piccolo,
Perché sia Joe che io abbiamo una certa affinità con l'Italia.
E ci sono stato ...
In questo granello di un paesino italiano,
Da dove mamma e papà hanno venuto,
Come quella pepita dal cielo,
E mi chiedo se è lo stesso che hanno lasciato ...
Mannaggia ... ma, mamma e papà erano ciechi?
Credo che le cose non sono sempre quelle che sembrano,
Perché è una maledizione essere il gatto che non prende mai il topo.
Allore ... arrividerci Campania e buon giorno ... Brum,
Sono così grato mamma e papà per aver deciso di venire nel Regno Unito,
Per cominciare una nuova vita, in un modo nuovo,
Perché se avessero deciso di rimanere,
Sarei a pascolare capre ora,
Con la mia conoscenza dell'agricoltura, che avrei acquisito,
Se il loro permesso di lavoro fosse scaduto,
O se avessero deciso di non far parte di quella manodopera migratoria,
Che ha fatto della mia mamma e del mio papa, stranieri in questa nazione.

E non lo sapevano ...

Quindi è "hi ho, hi ho - è al lavoro vanno"
Trattolo male è un terrone, trattala male è una maccherone.
È stata dura cercare lavoraro e imparare una lingua,
Quando tutto ciò che voi è pane per fare un panino.
Poi arriviamo noi, i figli, e sono giorni di scuola di nuovo,
Le suore cattoliche cambiano i nostri nomi, perché "Giovanni non va bene ...
Noi lo chiamiamo ... "John"... è molto più facile da dire,
E 'quello che è nella traduzione in lingua inglese,
Lo potete chiamare come vi piace a casa vostra,
Ma come dicono gli italiani ..."quando sei a Roma".

No ... non piangere, non passare i fazzoletti,
Perché mi chiedo se Joe, abbia dovuto affrontare gli stessi problemi
Se sia stato deriso nel suo vicinato,
Grazie a Enoch Powell ed ai suoi "fiumi di sangue".

Comunque ... svanisce Giovanni, ma "John" lavoro duro in classe,
Testa bassa e studiare, sperando di passare i miei esami.
Quindi, quali erano i piani di mamma e papà?
Beh, non volevano che seguissi le loro tracce −
Lunghe ore, duro lavoro, sudando sangue, rompendo la schiena.

(Detto in dialetto "Foianese". Foiano di Valfortore - il paese di mamma e papà)

"Lavor' cu le cerevel' ...pigli' a pay-a buon
E stibi nu poco di sold' pe' quando piogi.
Pigli 'na bella casa ... pigli 'na bella macchina
E non perd' u tempo a suon' a chitarra."

Ecco, questo è quasi quello che ho fatto
È per questo che sono qui,
Per rendere omaggio a due pilastri, che mi è caro.
La definizione dell'asse intorno a cui ruotano,
È nel loro coraggio, nella loro forza e nella loro determinazione.

My Heritage ... Innit?

To resemble someone of stature,
Or to capture a feature that rouses rapture,
Could be classed as a wonderful thing...
Perhaps you're the picture of Martin Luther King?
...Or John Lennon or Ghandi, Kate Bush or Bob Marley ...
Me? I look a bit like the great ... Joe Pasquale.
But that's okay – he's a nice guy,
So don't try and belittle me,
'Cause both Joe and I have an affinity with Italy.

And I've been there –
That speck of an Italian village where mom and dad came from,
Like that nugget from heaven
And I'm wondering if it's the same one
That they left behind – Jeeze ... were mom and dad blind?
Though I guess things are not always quite what they seem,
'Cause it's a bitch being the cat that never gets the cream.
So "arividerci Campania" and "buon giorno Brum"
I'm so grateful mom and dad had decided to come - to the UK,
To start a new life in a new way,
'Cause if they'd decided to stay, I could have been herding goats now
With my farming know how, which I would have acquired,
Had their work permits expired,
Or they'd chosen not to be part of that labour migration,
That made my mom and dad foreigners in this nation.

And didn't they know it.

So it's hi ho, hi ho - it's off to work they go,
Treat him hard he's a wop, treat her rough she's a daygo.
It was tough trying to work and pick up a language
When all you want is 'panini' to make-a da sandwich.
Then us kids come along and it's school days anew,
The Catholic nuns change our names, 'Cause "Giovanni won't do
"We'll call him John it's much easier to say,
It's what the English translation is, anyway,
You can call him what you like in your own home,
But as you eye-talians say ... 'when in Rome'.

No ... don't shed a tear, don't pass round the tissues,
'Cause I'm wondering if Joe had to face the same issues ...
Of funny name taunts in his neighbourhood,
Thanks to Enoch Powell and his rivers of blood.

Anyway ... Giovanni fades, but John works hard in class
Heads down and study and hope that I pass ... my exams,
So what were mom and dad's plans?
Well, they didn't want me following in their tracks -
Long hours, hard labour, sweating blood, breaking their backs.
(read in Italian accent) "Wek with-a you brain, getta good pay
An' sev a bita money for da rainy day,
Get-a nice-a house anna get-a nice car
Anna don west too much-a time with-a play da guitar"

So that's nearly what I did and that's really why I'm here,
To pay homage to two stalwarts and all, I hold dear.
The definition of the axis upon which I revolve,
Is down to their courage, their strength and resolve.

Letter to Birmingham

Dear Birmingham,

Somewhere between pre pubescent intoxication
And the Broad Street slags that became the new generation
Of mothers and fathers,
A blurred family of be-cycled helmets
Are unfazed by the fenced off funfair that fun forgot.

So they just kept going,
Never really knowing whether this was just another act
Of wanton neglect that they had grown to expect,
Or whether, Birmingham, like so many other things ...
You were going to get round to it ... sometime ... soon ... honest.

You see Birmingham,
You hadn't put any money in the meter for months,
Turning it in to a health and safety hazard,
Sodden in winter, awaiting the blizzard.
And somewhere in your Birmingham air,
A Morrissey melody makes its way down from Manchester.
Not everyday is like Sunday everywhere,
But today ... in this and a few more corners of the city ... it was.

Racing cars had been impounded,
Spaceships and rockets were grounded
And the novelty merry-go-round sounded sorry for itself
As it drowned in its unrelenting hushes ...
No laughing ...
No playing ...
No adrenalin rushes.

But there were blue skies once Birmingham,
As blue as a Saturday afternoon at St. Andrews.
And win or lose you're still free to choose the avenues
That lead to our sunshine within ...
Cue cello strings and violins, ELO's and Jeff Lynns
One love ends as another begins
And your sins are forgiven, your slate wiped clean,
Short memories forget where you had once been.

And you have been in love Birmingham ... I know you have,
Because you've seen the stars reflect in your reservoirs,
But you've also seen new born calves
Slaughtered in your abattoirs,
Been a bystander and stood by on faux pas,
Crashed into parked cars and walked away from the scene,
Neglecting to wipe your arse coming out of the latrine...
... you daft bastard.

Birmingham ... we're splayed out resplendent on your bed,
Like a party frock on prom night,
Waiting for you to grab our love handles
And rodger us to within an inch of our lives.
But sometimes ... you're as limp as a lettuce in a desert,
As flaccid as a ninety year old stoner on acid, drunk on gin,
Sometimes ... you just can't thumb it in.
Sometimes ... you babble like a brook
When you could rage like a river,
Sometimes ... you're like a dodgy UPS truck ...
You just don't deliver.

But Birmingham, I will always continue to give you my all.
Every mess of excess and thoughtless shortfall,
You've been maimed and mauled but remain immortal,
The welcome mat at the door for every beck and call.
There was always room at your Inn for my dad and mum
Yes Brum, it didn't matter where they came from,
You shot and bombed them in one decade,
Then helped them out in the next one.

You've been butchered by the country, heckled and harassed,
Broken tools and triple heart bypassed,
Forced to be the underclass
Just because of the way you speak.
And you know it's bleak when
Elocution electrocution treatment is a must,
Or be defined by your accent ... shit or bust.
But I trust you Birmingham.
I trust your half cut grins and gin soaked whims
That swim like breeze blocks in speedos.
But we know you've been short changed, slightly deranged
And never fully fulfilled your function
They interchanged you ... like spaghetti junction – them bastards.

Shiny,
Shitty,
Shoddy,
"Cum on feel the noise" said Noddy.
Dodgy scores and Ozzy Osbourne's roars,
Pouring scorn aboard profanity's shoulders,
But nobody told us you were catching boulders
Fired from Tolkien's catapults,
Where far canals get closer on aqueducts.

Shires were born on your hills and mills,
Giving birth to middle earth,
You read the books of countless towers and crystal palaces,
Took gulps from poisoned chalices and flaccid fallacies,
Handed down by the lying limbs of bastards' calluses,
You really know what malice is...
But I still can't resist yer...
You're slightly taboo ... like my best friend's sister.

Birmingham, don't listen when them bastards start dissin'
'Cause I love you more with three or four marbles missing.
They tell me you have lied, but I don't believe a word,
As town council after town council
Polishes and paints turds
Before shitting out new ones
And a million Gary Newbons will laugh at the sport
Of a hundred councillors that have sold you short – them bastards.

And they used to say you were a city of a thousand trades,
Most of which are now "streamlined" or "out sourced",
Forced out by bean counters and gaffers who were paid off
Then let off like Barabas,
Leaving you and your people with the abacus
To count the real cost,
And for every skill and resource lost and tossed into landfill
You ... our Mother of Invention will give birth to ten more ...
Some maybe still born ... some are feral yet fragile
Some are live and kicking,
Frantically flipping the bird to all who say ...
"But aren't you from that City?"
Yes I fucking am you bastards.

I'm of you and from you Birmingham
And I'll keep hitting them as long as you keep serving them
Swerving them balls around walls beyond keepers' reaches
'Till our features are rich like the suns of beaches.

Beautiful Brum, keep cocking a deaf 'un
To them bastards who think you need teaching a lesson
They get thrills to instil you with fear and distress an'
They're just cold meat ... you're the delicatessen.

So Birmingham, when them bastards try to tell you
That you're the dog shit stuck on their shoe
Tell them that you won't wash off,

Tell them you're the trash can full of untold gems,
Tell them you're the dandelion flower amidst their bouquet stems...
Tell them you'll keep getting up
After every punch in the guts or kick to the nuts,
Tell them that you just don't give a fuck.

Laughing with your yellowed teeth,
Laughing like the bullied boy
Who stands up high when bullets fly,
'Cause he's way past caring ...
Laughing like the mad beggar who has two tenths of fuck all
Yet still insists on sharing.

Laughing long,
Laughing loud,
Laughing proud ... at them bastards.

Losing It

For thirty five years he was that man,
That man who'd get up some time after six
And take his biggest risk – cornflakes or wheatabix?

That man who fell out of bed and fell into work
And though, sometimes, it would drive him berserk,
He drove his Ford into a car park full of Beamers and Mercs,
Offices full of suited jerks with hands up skirts of the junior clerks,
His head full of failure ... it would often hurt.

His wife had long ... since ... gone.
Found someone whose head wasn't screwed on so tight,
Took her out at night just so they could spend time together,
The guy wasn't big or clever, he was just ... there. He cared.
He broke up her monotony with his verve and spontaneity
Cradled her in his bassinet arms in her moments of frailty,
He saw so many things her husband had failed to see.

The kids had grown and flown the nest
The best part of two years previous
To his wife discovering her new found genius.
It was like her purpose for staying had gone when the kids had
And her life had turned a bit sad,
Since the spark had died for her kids' dad.
Which, in all honesty, had happened years before the kids left.
He was a moron marooned and a beggar bereft.
His pallet of music had been treble cleft beyond repair.

And all he could do was stare ...
And watch her ship sail ...
And feel his life fail ... as his cabin became water logged ...
And his days became groundhogged ...

But today ... was going to be different ...

All this time he'd been doing a job that he thought was a career,
And it was blatantly clear
That he was never going to get there ...from here.
Here ... where nobody's shit smelled
Here ... where his surname was always fucking mis-spelled
Here ... where loyalty and service are just pissed on,
Here ... where you can't smell a rat until you've kissed one.

Some said they should have seen it coming,
Some said it was no surprise,
Others tried to demonise when they realised
Their ignorance and lack of compassion
May have nurtured the worm that turned on the corpses that fed it,
May have written the pages of the book that blew up
In the hands of those that read it.

Nobody saw the light at the end of his tunnel go out,
Nor ask what his silent tears were all about,
Nobody saw him burst into flame,
In the same way that nobody took the time
To learn or call him by his first name.

And nobody forgot what he did that day ...
And nobody would remain unscathed,
And the blame was tossed and the buck was passed
And the rueful shuffled ... whenever questions were asked.

Valentine's Day in the Jungle

I hear stories.

Stories of a sinking ship that can carry no more ...
Can't make it ashore 'cause it's packed to the brim
Where conditions are poor and pickings are slim,
It sounds grim ... but while sailors squabble
Over scraps and squeezed spaces,
The opulent officers wear grins on their faces,
As they drill holes of austerity in the hull
Whilst reciting their well rehearsed mantra ... "the ship is full".
Yet, they swing fat cats and gorge in their enormous quarters,
Building barbed wire barriers,
Instead of bridges over waters ...
Exporters of war and slaughter to order,
With a barrage of broad sides on a biased border.

I see stories.

I see stories of hope and resilience,
Where others are told to see fear and ambivalence,
The threat of disobedience and an assault on sensibilities...
Just pathetic excuses for continued hostilities.
I see frozen faces with the warmest smiles,
Where others are told to see rapists and paedophiles.
I see the cost of ignorance and neglect,
People paying high prices,
Where others are told to see terrorists,
Told to devour divisive devices ... so why alarms and why surprises,
When a doorstep challenge becomes a crisis?

I see families who have cried so many tears, they have none left,
One time blessed though now bereft
On Calais' coastline as unwelcome guests.
So how apt and fitting it is,
That those benevolent French authorities
See refugees with tearless eyes, blood shot and raw
So provide them with canisters filled with more.

I tell stories

I tell stories 'till I'm hoarse, but is anyone listening?
Compassion's gone missing
And right wing rhetoric resolve is stiffening,
It's as crippling as Annie Wilkes in 'Misery'
Yet Joseph marches on, in the midst of this artillery.
He's here because he's sure metaphors won't kill
As quickly as the civil war in West Sudan will.
This once proud man tells me of his plight in 'Pidgin English'
It's left him morally molested and pigeon chested,
Says he'll swim the channel if he has to, once he's fully rested
From his last attempt at stowing away ...
So we drink tea together on Valentine's Day.

And I make no apology and refuse to say sorry
When I say the best thing to come out of France ... right now ...
Would be a thousand hopeful smiles on the back of a lorry,
A humane quarry and a ferry full of hope, not hate to fill our soul,
With an open gate ... at border control.
Because these are the sad and selfish days
Where we need to over-stand open gates ... work both ways ...
There's a whole globe waiting for the xenophobe,
Good riddance to bad rubbish please!
Because I can't think of a fairer trade,
Than fascists for refugees.

Spoz Introduces ...

Davanté Dunkley. You bump into some really cool and interesting people whilst shopping in Morrison's, near Longbridge and Davante is one such person. Having chatted briefly, he came along to a night I run with Maggie Doyle and Fergus McGonigall called "Licensed to Rhyme" in Barnt Green, near Birmingham. I was instantly struck by his voice, obviously something you can't appreciate by reading his work in here! But not only that, his subject matter took me by surprise ... in a good way.

Why?
by Davanté Dunkley

If life is a game then each day you need progression,
It seems like our identities nowadays only lie in our profession,
So if you don't have one, does that mean your life isn't a blessing?
There are so many theories, I guess until death, we'll be guessing.

Asking, what am I here for?
To work and pay tax?
Wait, we had God given gifts before this government,
So there has to be more to that.

An Atheist told me the stars,
A Buddhist told me peace,
Christians say Jesus died for our sins,
So we can choose who we want to be.

Here's another question ...
Why are there so many different religions?
Is there more than one God, that sends us here on different missions?
Or is it all one God, built from all our ancestors' different visions?

But seeming none of us really know, why do we fight over this?
I guess our pride, and ego get in the way,
They do say ignorance,
Is bliss,
But, are there not more important things to worry about than this,
Like all these stabbings,
And kids, killing kids,

Was it the fruit Adam and Eve bit, that released this toxic pride?
We are told as little boys to man up, it's only women that can cry,
That leaves us men broken,
Lost, with nowhere to confide,
If that's the wave that drowns this nation, I refuse to ride that tide.

There are so many questions, and most, lead to violence,
If there is power in words, why don't we use our tongues, like tridents?
Become the rulers of our lives, and build people up with words?
Instead of holding people down, we can choose to fly like birds.

Build our own dreams,
Let's soar, like an Eagle,
But we can't do that, if we're not around the right people,

That's why I think you should look at life like a test,
What do you reckon?
It's why I'm in this mirror,
Staring at 2 pupils,
Trying to teach them a better lesson.

Spoz Introduces ...

Jemima Hughes. Out of the blue, this slightly nervous and edgy person turns up to "Licensed to Rhyme". "Would you like an open mic slot?" I ask. "Erm ... okay. I haven't really done anything like this before", she replies. Boom. BOOM!! Storm Jemima well and truly piled into Licensed to Rhyme that night. Must have been a couple of years ago now and since then, Jemima has been ripping the roof off many a poetry night and winning the occasional poetry slam too. She is brutal and beautiful and honest and it's a privilege to introduce her to you.

Tornado
by Jemima Hughes

The National Weather Service has issued a severe weather warning, storm Jemima has hit the south. A tornado, intensity warning F3, is set to tear through your life, turn everything on its head, emotions will be rife, this weather warning is most certainly a code red.

Prepare to feel a surge of adrenaline,
awaken your every sense
with her first presence.
Try not to be tense.
Remember she doesn't mean to cause offence.
She is as natural as mountains or the moon's mere existence,
but with natural follows disaster,
don't fall victim to her false pretence.

You're going to bind in a whirlwind of heart pounding excitement
and fear of devastation.
Please beware of her irresistible fixation,
on you.
She will cling to you,
she will consume you,

she will rip off your roof leaving you exposed to who knows who,
because she believes it could be good for you.

You being at the centre of her
should not be confused with you having a life of your own,
to which you should retreat.
She will drop you back down to the ground
alongside your hail stricken heartbeat.
How is it you feel complete,
when your heart is debris
drowning on concrete?

Her aggression was not meant for you.
No one wants to be a disaster,
no matter how natural.
It accumulated inside of her and she blew
spine chilling surface winds in to your eyes.
Blindingly beautiful skies,
disturbed by cries
to go back in time.

Power flashes from lines
light the way for broken futures to collide.

If you're brave enough to cut off the air supply
the vortex will weaken.
Roping out,
tornado choked with doubt
of her existence.
Becoming a thin cut out
of her former self.
Trees creak as they straighten their backs to watch her dissipate.

You won't see the same her again.
Don't forget after the storm will come a rainbow.
A rainbow to frame
the lasting impression that became,
all that remained
of the life threatening game she played.

How colourful it is,
Is up to you.

Spoz Introduces ...

Tom McCann. I first met Tom eating chips in Rubery Park whilst he was busking for salt and vinegar. Impressed with his simultaneous guitar and spoon playing skills, I naturally asked him if he was any good at poetry (naturally). And he naturally was. All silliness aside, I have been nothing but impressed with Tom's writing, delivery and enthusiasm for poetry and spoken word. He even runs his own night now, called "Spoken Trend" in Kings Norton, Birmingham. I've watched him grow and I know he's going to keep growing.

Making Peace With Your Own Patch
by Tom McCann

The grass is so much greener over there,
That's because they have the better weather over there,
A larger lawn to be mown
And in the morn the dew is just that little bit dew-ier.

The stars are a little bit shinier over there,
That's because they've got less of that light pollution, polluting the air,
So, when you wish upon one, you'd better make it a good one,
As it will come true.

Opportunity is always knocking over there,
Little surprises here and there,
A roll of the dice, with eyes half closed,
And they just won't stop rolling before they land on a perfect score.

There's none of this wishing the seasons away over there,
There's reassurance in tradition and routine,
And it would be nice to be blissfully unaware,
Because then you don't see, then there's no way of knowing.

There's not the feeling of being cheated over there,
Recognizing that this is it, yet finding solace in that fact,
Not falling into disrepair and being consumed by it,
But maneuvering through the madness to find the still.

There's a sense of focusing on one's own surroundings over there,
Not poking your head over the garden fence to stare,

And see the neighbour's lawn through a pair of emerald tinted glasses,
Making peace with your own patch.

And slowing things down,
And getting rid,
And seeing things through,
To the end, over there.

ACKNOWLEDGEMENTS

This is a list of people who have inspired me, influenced me or helped me in anyway (whether they know it or not). So allow me to say "thank you".

Mama e Papa e la famiglia Esposito
Zack, Fran and Claude xxx
Dreadlockalien, Elvis McGonagall, Bowie, AF Harrold, John Hegley, John Cooper Clarke, Attila the Stockbroker, Hollie McNish, Kate Tempest, Polar Bear, Rob Gee, Berko, Andy Craven Griffiths, Longfella, Jimmy Davis, Johnny Fluffypunk, Jess Green, Keiron King, The Antipoet, Pete the Temp, Jodi Anne Bickley, Hannah Teasdale, Bohdan Piasecki, Leon Priestnall, Matt Windle, Holly Daffurn, Helen Gregory, Charley Barnes, Ash Dickinson, Jamie Thrasivoulou, Steve Pottinger, Dave Pitt and Fergus McGonigall.
The brilliant Ten Letters crew, namely ...
Lorna Meehan, Aliyah Hasinah, Aliyah Denton, Callum Bate, Melissa Bate, Maggie Doyle, Nyanda Foday, Jasmine Gardosi, Hazel Sealeaf, Sipho Eric Dube, Luci Hammans, Casey Bailey, Emma Pursehouse (again!), Joe Cook, Hannah Silva, Zack and Stringy P (and Jord!).
Everyone in the Brum poetry scene, especially Amerah Saleh, Kamil Mahmood, Lexia Tomlinson, Nafeesa Hamid, Tom McCann, Sean Colletti,
The ever changing Brum Uni crew, Stuart Bartholomew (cheers dude!) Jemima Hughes, Hannah Swingler, Jimmy Fantastic and Big Bren.
Anisa and the Beatfreeks Collective crew,
Poetry on Loan (nice one Brenda!),
Birmingham, Worcestershire, Shropshire and Staffordshire Libraries, Steve Wilson, Elaine Knight and Worcestershire (Severn) Arts crew, Jonathan and Writing West Midlands,

Arts Council West Midlands (cheers James!)
Marcus and Sara-Jane,
Apples and Snakes especially Jacob and Lisa (and the rest of you obviously!),
Birmingham Youth Service,
Women and Theatre,
The Palace Theatre in Redditch,
Artrix Theatre in Bromsgrove,
MAC Birmingham,
Authors Abroad (you rock!)
John Davenport and Kirk Andrews for their amazing works of art.
Paul Stringer for his bostin photography.
Leni Remedios for helping with the translations.
All the schools I've visited and yet to visit, especially the teachers who have been brilliantly supportive under stress and all the kids who have been ace, even though they thought (and probably still think) "poetry's boring".

...and anyone else who knows me.

ABOUT VERVE POETRY PRESS

Verve Poetry Festival is a new press focussing intently on meeting a local need in Birmingham - a need for the vibrant poetry scene here in Brum to find a way to present itself to the poetry world via publication. Co-founded by Stuart Bartholomew and Amerah Saleh, it is publishing poets from all corners of the city - poets that represent the city's varied and energetic qualities and will communicate its many poetic stories.

Added to this is a colourful pamphlet series featuring poets who have previously performed at our sister festival - and a poetry show series which captures the magic of longer poetry performance pieces by poets such as Polarbear and Matt Abbott.

Like the festival, we will strive to think about poetry in inclusive ways and embrace the multiplicity of approaches towards this glorious art.

www.vervepoetrypress.com
@VervePoetryPres
mail@vervepoetrypress.com